Black Wednesday

A Re-examination of Britain's Experience in the
Exchange Rate Mechanism

Black Wednesday

A Re-examination of Britain's Experience in the Exchange Rate Mechanism

ALAN BUDD

THIRTY-FOURTH WINCOTT LECTURE
5 OCTOBER 2004

WITH COMMENTARIES BY
DEREK SCOTT
TIM CONGDON
SAMUEL BRITTAN

The Institute of Economic Affairs

First published in Great Britain in 2005 by
The Institute of Economic Affairs
2 Lord North Street
Westminster
London SW1P 3LB
in association with Profile Books Ltd

The mission of the Institute of Economic Affairs is to improve public understanding of the fundamental institutions of a free society, with particular reference to the role of markets in solving economic and social problems.

A CIP catalogue record for this book is available from the British Library.

ISBN 0 255 36566 7

Many IEA publications are translated into languages other than English or are reprinted. Permission to translate or to reprint should be sought from the Director General at the address above.

Typeset in Stone by MacGuru Ltd
info@macguru.org.uk

Printed and bound in Great Britain by Hobbs the Printers

CONTENTS

THE AUTHOR

Sir Alan Budd has been Provost of the Queen's College, Oxford, since 1999. He was previously a member of the Bank of England's Monetary Policy Committee and was Chief Economic Adviser to the Treasury from 1991 to 1997.

He was educated at the London School of Economics and Cambridge University. His academic career has included posts at the London Business School, Southampton University, Carnegie-Mellon University, Pittsburgh (Ford Foundation Visiting Professor), and the University of New South Wales (Reserve Bank of Australia Visiting Professor).

He is a governor of the National Institute for Economic and Social Research and the Institute for Fiscal Studies, an executive editor of *World Economics* and a member of the editorial advisory board of the *Oxford Review of Economic Policy*.

Sir Alan was chairman of the Gambling Review Body and a member of the Committee to Review the Future Funding of the BBC and of the Independent Panel on BBC Charter Renewal. He is a senior adviser to Credit Suisse First Boston and a consultant to the G7 Group. He was knighted in 1997.

FOREWORD

The Wincott Memorial Lectures, which have been held every year since 1970, provide an opportunity for distinguished economists and practitioners to reflect on topics that lie at the centre of the debate about economic policy. Sir Alan Budd's 2004 lecture, which is published together with three commentaries in this book, is unusual in that it focuses on a particular episode in Britain's recent economic history – entry into, and departure from, the Exchange Rate Mechanism (ERM) of the European Monetary System in 1990–92. That episode remains a source of lively debate, both in terms of domestic politics and in relation to the wider issue of how best to keep inflation under control.

Most commentators have regarded 'Black Wednesday' – the day on which Britain left the ERM – as a humiliation for the Conservative government and an indictment of its economic management over the preceding five or six years. Thus, in reviewing the Conservatives' economic record in his 1997 Wincott Lecture, Professor Nicholas Crafts gave them high marks for what they had achieved in microeconomic policy, particularly in the field of competition and labour market reform. But their Achilles heel, he argued, was macroeconomic management. They had made 'major errors' which had led to 'excessive economic fluctuations and the eventual loss of the government's reputation for economic competence'.

That mistakes were made in the late 1980s and early 1990s is not in dispute, and many people (often with the benefit of hindsight) include in those mistakes the decision to join the ERM. But there is another way of looking at that experience, and in his lecture Sir Alan provides a closely reasoned case for believing that the outcome of the ERM adventure was a blessing rather than a disaster. The argument is that, without ERM membership, it would have been very difficult to squeeze inflation out of the system, and that departure from the ERM led to a new approach to monetary policy which, by 'locking in' low inflation, paved the way for an exceptionally long period of economic stability. According to this account, the decision by the incoming Labour government in 1997 to delegate interest rate management to the Monetary Policy Committee of the Bank of England was not so much a radical change as an extension of the policies introduced by the Conservatives in the post-ERM period.

Could inflation have been brought under control in other ways, as it was in countries such as Australia and New Zealand? Was resort to the ERM, as Martin Wolf has suggested in the *Financial Times,* a reflection of the defeatism of British officialdom – the belief that Britain was incapable of achieving stability without outside help?

These and other aspects of Sir Alan's argument are discussed in this monograph by three economists – Sir Samuel Brittan, Professor Tim Congdon and Derek Scott. There are disagreements between them on several points – not least on whether the UK should have joined the ERM in the mid-1980s, or whether, as Professor Congdon argues, the fatal decision at that time was to abandon money supply targets as the principal anti-inflationary weapon. We believe that bringing their disparate viewpoints together in a single volume, along with Sir Alan's lecture, will contribute to a better understanding of the ERM episode and illuminate, if only indirectly, the very different issues raised by Britain's possible membership of European Monetary Union.

The trustees of the Wincott Foundation are grateful to Sir Alan for agreeing to deliver the 2004 Wincott Lecture, and to Sir Samuel Brittan, Professor Tim Congdon and Derek Scott for commenting on it.

SIR GEOFFREY OWEN
Chairman of the Trustees,
The Wincott Foundation
April 2005

LLANBEDR

Victoria Inn ★★★ INN ♉

LL45 2LD ☎ **01341 241213** 📄 **01341 241644**
e-mail: junevicinn@aol.com
web: www.victoriainnllanbedr.co.uk
dir: *On A496 between Barmouth and Harlech*

Fascinating features for pub connoisseurs are the circular wooden settle, ancient stove, grandfather clock and flagged floors in the bar of the Victoria. Home-made food is served in the lounge bar and restaurant, complemented by a range of Robinson's ales. The children's play area in the garden has a playhouse, slides and swings. The Rhinog mountain range and famous Roman Steps are right on the doorstep.

Open all day all wk 11-11 (Sun noon-10.30) **Bar Meals** Av main course £9 food served all day **Restaurant** Fixed menu price fr £10.50 food served all day ⊕ FREDERIC ROBINSON ◀ Robinson's Best Bitter, guest bitters ♂ Stowford Press. ♉ 10 **Facilities** Children's menu Play area Dogs allowed Garden Parking Rooms 5

TUDWEILIOG

Lion Hotel ♉

LL53 8ND ☎ **01758 770244**
e-mail: martinlee1962@hotmail.com
dir: *A487 from Caernarfon onto A499 towards Pwllheli. Right onto B4417 to Nefyn, onto Edern then onto Tudweiliog*

The beach is only a mile away from this friendly inn, run by the Lee family for over 30 years. The large garden and children's play area makes the pub especially popular with the cyclists, walkers and families who flock to the Lleyn Peninsula. The bar features an extensive list of over 80 malt whiskies. A typical menu might consist of Tuscan bean soup, Welsh lamb bake, and rice pudding.

Open all wk **Bar Meals** L served all wk 12-2 D served all wk 6-9 Av main course £8.25 ⊕ FREE HOUSE ◀ Purple Moose Brewery Ale, Boddingtons. ♉ 6 **Facilities** Children's menu Play area Family room Garden Parking

MONMOUTHSHIRE

ABERGAVENNY

Clytha Arms ♉

Clytha NP7 9BW ☎ **01873 840209** 📄 **01873 840209**
e-mail: theclythaarms@tiscali.co.uk
dir: *From A449/A40 junction (E of Abergavenny) follow signs for 'Old Road Abergavenny/Clytha'*

Andrew and Beverley Canning have now celebrated 30 years of marriage, 18 of which have been spent at the Clytha. They are as enthusiastic as ever about their hostelry, despite the trials and tribulations of the weather and the economy. This former dower house is heavily involved with the Welsh Cider Festival in May and the Beer and Cheese Festival in August. Hardly surprising then that the bar offers Weston ciders and the Clytha's own perry, as well as local beers from the Rhymney Brewery and Crow Valley – at least four are always on offer. Whisky, gin and vodka come from the Penderyn Distillery just 20 miles away. As for food, Andrew cooks up a storm on his new oak-fired grill, starting the day by baking his own bread and muffins. The menu offers treats for every taste, from rabbit and cider pie to bacon, laverbread and cockles. Treacle pudding and home-made custard to finish is a must.

Open noon-3 6-mdnt (Fri-Sun noon-mdnt) Closed: 25 Dec, Mon L **Bar Meals** L served Tue-Sun 12.30-2.30 D served Mon-Sat 7-9.30 Av main course £10 **Restaurant** L served Tue-Sun 12.30-2.30 D served Mon-Sat 7-9.30 Fixed menu price fr £16.95 Av 3 course à la carte fr £25 ⊕ FREE HOUSE ◀ Felinfoel Double Dragon, Rhymney Bitter, 4 guest ales (300+ per year) ♂ Westons Old Rosie, Westons Perry, Clytha Perry. ♉ 10 **Facilities** Children's menu Play area Dogs allowed Garden Parking

Wales

ACKNOWLEDGEMENTS

I am most grateful to Mervyn King for his valuable comments on an earlier draft of this lecture.

Black Wednesday

A Re-examination of Britain's Experience in the
Exchange Rate Mechanism

1 BLACK WEDNESDAY – A RE-EXAMINATION OF BRITAIN'S EXPERIENCE IN THE EXCHANGE RATE MECHANISM

Alan Budd

Introduction

The objective of this Wincott Lecture is to re-examine the events associated with the UK's brief membership of the Exchange Rate Mechanism (ERM) of the European Monetary System. I am interested in the experience itself but I also want to examine its effect on the performance of the UK economy. The commonly held view is that our membership of the ERM was a disaster and was always doomed to fail. I shall seek to demonstrate that, although it was certainly a political catastrophe, the case can be made that it was an economic triumph and marked the turning point in our macro-economic performance.

A tale of two economies

As a way of introducing the case that is explained in detail below, it is instructive to consider two unnamed economies and some statistics that present a fairly conventional way of measuring the performance of an economy over an eleven-year period.[1] The economies will be described as 'Economy A' and 'Economy B'. Economy A is an economy that had periods of rapid growth

---

1   Charts illustrating these points are shown in Budd (2004).

but very large swings in growth and, sometimes, large swings in output. The eleven-year period started with a recession and ended with another. Economy B, however, is remarkably stable. Growth is positive in every single one of the eleven years and, for most of the period, growth stays at between about 2 and 4 per cent a year. Economy A has high unemployment throughout the eleven years. There is a brief period when unemployment falls but it soon reverts to its previous peak. Economy B starts with high unemployment but it falls steadily and stays at low levels from about year eight onwards. With regard to inflation, Economy A starts with inflation at about 12 per cent. It falls to below 4 per cent but this success is not sustained and it rises to about 10 per cent before falling back again to about 4 per cent. Economy B has inflation which is low and stable, staying at between 2 and 3.5 per cent for almost the entire period.

So if one had to choose between these two economies one might reasonably conclude that Economy B had performed far better than Economy A. It has more stable growth, lower unemployment and lower, and more stable, inflation. Which are these two economies? Economy A and Economy B are both the UK economy, Economy A being the UK economy in the first half of the period, from 1981 to 2003, and Economy B being the UK economy in the second half. This analysis does not prove anything, but it is clear that the British economy has generally performed better in the last ten years than it did in the previous decade. I shall explore the part that ERM membership played in that record.

I shall start by reminding you of the events preceding ERM membership. Then I shall discuss the experience of being in the ERM and the circumstances that led to our departure from it. Then I shall talk about our economic performance since leaving the ERM and see how far I can support the claim that ERM membership deserves a large share of the credit for it.

Economic developments in the years before ERM entry

The election of a Conservative government in 1979 may seem the obvious starting point for an analysis of economic developments before ERM entry. More significant, though, was the combination, in 1975, of inflation at 30 per cent and unemployment at then record post-World War II levels. That combination was experienced under a Labour government, but was the consequence of policies introduced during the earlier Conservative administration under Edward Heath. Those policies involved the use of fiscal measures to cut unemployment (with considerable short-run success) while using direct controls on pay and prices in an attempt to control inflation. For reasons I have discussed elsewhere (Budd, 2002), economic events in 1970 and 1971 led the government to believe that an expansion of demand would help, rather than hinder, the objective of cutting inflation.

The abandonment of the post-war tradition of demand management was announced in a notable speech by James Callaghan, in September 1976. But while it seemed clear that crude Keynesianism – which was so crude that it was hardly Keynesian at all – was wrong, it was not so obvious what should replace it. Joining the ERM in October 1990 can be thought of as yet another attempt to find an answer.

Earlier attempts included monetary targets, which, as some have forgotten, were first introduced by a Labour Chancellor of the Exchequer but which gained rather greater prominence under the Conservatives. After 1980, monetary targets were accompanied by a planned path for the public sector borrowing requirement – one part of the policy framework which has survived even if the details have changed. The experiment in seeking to control inflation by setting quantitative monetary targets did not match the hopes of its most enthusiastic supporters, among whom I was one. Inflation was reduced, from 20 per cent in 1980 to 5 per cent by 1985; but the monetary growth outcomes bore little relation to the targets. Between 1980 and 1982, the money supply grew twice as fast as it was supposed to but, as we would now recognise, monetary conditions were exceptionally tight. GDP fell in 1980 and 1981 and, although it started to grow from 1982 onwards, unemployment continued to rise until 1986, reaching a peak of over 3 million unemployed.

The philosophy behind the new approach to policy-making was set out in Nigel Lawson's Mais Lecture of 1984. He argued that previously policy had suffered from what economists would call an assignment error. Instruments were wrongly assigned to objectives. In the past, he argued, microeconomic instruments (price and wage controls, for example) had been used to control inflation and macroeconomic instruments, particularly changes in the fiscal balance, had been used to control unemployment and the growth of output. Conservative economic policy reversed that assignment. There are few who would quarrel with that analysis, though support for incomes policies as a means of reducing inflation persisted for some time; but the problem, at least on the macroeconomic side, was implementation. In particular there were the problems of how to select quantitative monetary targets and what to do about the exchange rate.

The Budgets from 1980 onwards included targets for the growth of the broad money supply. From 1982 onwards they were accompanied by targets for the growth of the narrow money supply.

Money supply targets were unsatisfactory because it was extremely difficult, if not impossible, to establish stable demand functions for money. The role of the exchange rate proved equally problematic. In its simplest version, the monetarist approach required setting an appropriate monetary target and allowing the exchange rate to float freely. If the exchange rate were not allowed to float freely, an important part of the transmission system, from the money supply to inflation, was lost. This part of the transmission system was thought to be particularly important in an open economy such as that of the UK.

In the early years of the new policy, the Treasury was willing to allow sterling to fluctuate freely. The rise in the exchange rate in 1979 and 1980, which no doubt reflected the de facto tightness of monetary policy, was one means by which real demand was slowed down and inflation was cut. One may suspect that it went farther than was comfortable and that the government hoped that the abolition of foreign exchange controls in 1980 would help bring the exchange rate down, though it didn't do so. In practice, while appreciation of the currency could be tolerated, depreciation seemed to be more of a problem. In February 1985, the pound fell very close to parity with the dollar. In his Budget speech in March of that year Nigel Lawson said:

> There are those who argue that if we stick to sound internal policies, the exchange rate can be left to take care of itself. In the long run that may well be true, but significant movements in the exchange rate, whatever their cause, can have a short-term impact on the general price level and on inflationary expectations. This process can acquire

a momentum of its own, making sound internal policies harder to implement. So benign neglect is not an option.

So much for free floating. The Budget of 1985 also came closer than before to announcing a target for money GDP (something for which Samuel Brittan had long argued). As Mr Lawson said, 'The Medium Term Financial Strategy is as firm a guarantee against inadequate money demand as it is against excessive monetary demand.'

So by 1985 we had a somewhat eclectic approach to macroeconomic policy – a bit of monetary targeting, a bit of money GDP targeting, and some concern for the exchange rate, though the broad money target was suspended later in the year.

We now know that there was a serious attempt in the autumn of 1985 to persuade Mrs Thatcher to join the ERM. To quote Nigel Lawson, 'The overwhelming case for joining now was the desirability of reinforcing our anti-inflationary strategy. While this continued so far to be successful, the monetary indicators were proving increasingly difficult to interpret.' Mrs Thatcher rejected the arguments outright, thereby producing what Nigel Lawson described as the saddest event of his time as Chancellor and the greatest missed opportunity (Lawson, 1992).

In the absence of ERM membership, Nigel Lawson sought, for a period in 1987/88, to stabilise sterling's exchange rate against the Deutschmark. This was in the general context of the move to stabilise exchange rates after the Louvre Accord. He has argued that this policy started with the objective of keeping sterling above its pre-Louvre level of DM2.8, but the market chose to guess that there was an upper limit and that it was DM3. During 1987/88, the policy of shadowing the Deutschmark required a series of interest rate cuts, and by May 1988 base rates were cut (briefly) to 7.5

per cent. With hindsight we can accept that this policy was over-stimulatory from around 1986 onwards. The exchange rate policy may have contributed to this error, though the general problem was of estimating the pressure on resources – had the economy become capacity constrained? At the time I shared the general optimism that it had not.

Once policy had turned, interest rates were raised rapidly, to 13 per cent by the end of 1988 and reaching 15 per cent in October 1989. They were held at that level for a year.

June 1989 saw the presentation of the so-called Madrid Conditions which had to be satisfied before the UK would join the ERM. The conditions were: lower inflation, the abandonment of exchange controls, further progress towards completion of the single market, free competition in financial services, and the strengthening of European competition policy.

On 5 October 1990 the Madrid Conditions were deemed to have been met and it was announced that the UK would join the ERM on the following Monday at a central parity of DM2.95 with a permitted band of 6 per cent either side. Headline inflation was 10.9 per cent. Inflation, as measured by retail prices excluding mortgage interest payments, was 9.5 per cent. That obviously did not meet the Madrid requirement that inflation should be lower (in fact it was a peak); but it was explained that the prospects were for lower inflation.

Whatever the political arguments regarding the ERM, the economic case for joining was that it would provide a more successful basis for macroeconomic policy, particularly counter-inflationary policy, than we had been able to achieve through independent domestic policies. It was, in a sense, an admission of failure. It had not proved possible to discover the correct combination of monetary and exchange rate targeting. The story had ended with a misjudgement of economic conditions. Inflation had briefly fallen below 3 per cent, helped by a fall in oil prices, but from 1986 onwards the economy had been allowed to grow too rapidly and inflation had, once again, reached double figures. In fact one might argue with hindsight that the policy response, though tardy, was correct and would have brought inflation under control, but an alternative approach to policy was thought necessary (see also below). The ERM gave the UK a 'nominal anchor', in the form of an exchange rate target, albeit with a wide band around it. The hope was that the nominal anchor would bring UK inflation in line with the lower rate prevailing among other ERM countries, particularly in Germany.

In the ERM

The period in the ERM and the events surrounding our departure from it have been much described, most notably in Philip Stephens's book *Politics and the Pound* (Stephens, 1997), and I shall sketch only the main economic developments.

Headline inflation was 10.9 per cent when we joined and 3.6 per cent when we left. The figures for the more reliable indicator of underlying inflation, known as RPIX, were respectively 9.5 per cent and 4 per cent. Interest rates were cut by 1 per cent to 14 per cent on the day we joined and were 10 per cent on the day before Black Wednesday. GDP fell by 1.4 per cent in 1991 and rose by 0.2 per cent in 1992. Unemployment (as measured by the claimant count) rose over the two years from 1.7 million to 2.8 million. Those are the bare facts: in crude terms, a policy-induced recession brought down inflation.

Although there had been people who opposed the policy right

from the beginning, popular opposition to the ERM, in the press and elsewhere, did not really get under way until the summer of 1992. Norman Lamont felt able to give a fairly confident Mansion House speech in the autumn of 1991, when he was able to draw attention to the fall in the inflation rate and to point out that the interest rate differential between the UK and Germany was at its lowest for ten years. The objections became much noisier as unemployment rose and there appeared to be no signs of economic recovery.

There has been a long debate about whether the problem in 1992 was the exchange rate or the level of interest rates. I now realise that the debate is misguided for two reasons. The first is that, if policy settings were too tight, it is not helpful to try to distinguish between the effects of two separate elements. If you are simultaneously being hit over the head with a shovel and your knees are being battered by a mallet you do not necessarily seek to ask which onslaught is causing the pain. Policy conditions would have been less tight had the exchange rate or interest rates been lower. But there is a particular point about the level of the exchange rate which I shall make below.

The second reason why the debate is misguided is that it assumes that policy was too tight. But who says so? We cannot consider whether or not policy was too tight unless we can answer the question 'Too tight for what objective?' We need to discover what the policy objectives were and then we can consider whether the policy settings were appropriate for meeting those objectives. The main objective of tight monetary policy was, presumably, to control inflation. The intermediate objective was to keep the UK in the ERM. Interest rates certainly weren't too high for the intermediate objective; if anything they were too low. I think that Philip

Stephens (ibid.) is right to emphasise the eventual consequences for the credibility of the ERM policy of failing to match the increase in German interest rates in December 1991 and then to cut them to 10 per cent in May 1992. Were interest rates too high for the control of inflation? That, of course, depends on what the inflation objective was. Unfortunately we cannot know the answer to that since, by joining the ERM, the government had sacrificed its ability to choose its own inflation rate. It was willing to make that sacrifice in the belief that the outcome of membership would be low and stable inflation. Thus its implicit inflation target was whatever was consistent with continued membership of the ERM. One ex post rationale for leaving when we did was that continued membership would lead to an inflation rate that was lower than thought necessary or desirable.

One question that I find extremely difficult to answer is whether in fact we could have stayed as a member of the ERM. All counter-factuals of this type present enormous problems. It is tempting to divide the question into two and to ask, first, could we have *avoided* the speculative attack on sterling and, second, could we have *survived* the speculative attack? But that division won't quite work since speculative attacks themselves depend on views about survival. History would no doubt have been different if other members of the ERM had been willing to support our efforts, but that pushes us back to the question of what actions of ours might have persuaded them to do so.

I have said that it is not sensible to ask whether the problem in 1992 was the interest rate or the exchange rate; but there is a question that is perhaps more sensible. It has been said that the Bundesbank, and particularly its president, Dr Schlesinger, believed that we had joined the ERM at too high an exchange rate. I want to comment briefly on that issue. Some of you may be aware that Samuel Brittan wrote a piece in the *Financial Times* (repeated in ibid.) claiming that Mervyn King and I visited Frankfurt on 14 September, the Monday before Black Wednesday, in an attempt to persuade the Bundesbank that sterling's exchange rate was sustainable. Let us assume, for the moment, that such a visit did take place. Was the exchange rate sustainable? I simply do not know how the Bundesbank's doubts about sterling's sustainability might have affected its actions on Black Wednesday. But it is remarkable that, although departure from the ERM was followed by a significant depreciation as sterling appeared to settle at around DM2.25 to DM2.50, since 1997 the rate seems to have settled, with remarkable stability, around DM2.95: the original central ERM rate.

While we were in the ERM, underlying inflation fell from 9.5 per cent to 4 per cent. Headline inflation fell from 10.9 per cent to 3.6 per cent. It is the reduction in inflation which I wish to emphasise. Membership of the ERM forced the UK to maintain the policies that brought inflation down to the levels at which it has stayed ever since. Norman Lamont, in the role of Ulysses, was tied to the mast, his ears stuffed with wax, so that he was unable to hear the siren calls for reflation.

Was ERM membership responsible for reducing inflation?

It is one thing to show that inflation fell while we were in the ERM, it is another to establish that it was ERM membership which was responsible. To illustrate this issue, I would rely on the model of inflation embodied in consensus models of the economy, with inflation depending on unemployment (or some measure of the output gap) and inflationary expectations. That approach is consistent with a variety of hypotheses about how inflationary expectations are formed and about the determinants of the growth of output and demand. The ideal policy for cutting inflation has a large effect on expectations and requires a low cost in terms of output forgone and jobs (temporarily) lost.

It is clear that inflation expectations did fall while we were in the ERM, though they rose again when we left, and the evidence supports the view that commitment to the ERM played a part in achieving that fall. That effect required our membership of ERM to have been credible, which appears to have been the case. Although public opposition to ERM membership became increasingly virulent as 1992 progressed, confidence in our membership, as revealed by the currency markets, was maintained until the last week of our membership.

So I do believe that membership of the ERM had counter-inflationary benefits that went beyond the deflationary policies required to sustain it. I do not rely on that result, however. The essential point is that policy was held tight for long enough to bring inflation down to current levels. The success of the ERM experiment depended not only on our membership, for slightly less than two years, but also on our leaving it when we did. Had we retained our membership at the DM2.95 central rate, we would have experienced further increases in unemployment, and although inflation would no doubt have fallen further, the price would not have been worth paying.

The policy of ERM membership was successful because the markets believed that we would maintain our membership of the ERM, so inflationary expectations fell. But it was a classic example of time inconsistency, of reneging on commitments. Were we ever to embark on a similar experiment in the future, markets might reasonably remember how we behaved last time. Also, it should be remembered that we did not leave at a time of our own choosing. I believe that we joined at the right time and left at the right time but that was a matter of luck rather than skill.

Could we have stayed in the ERM? This leads to another unanswerable question about the final period. Suppose, as many argued was appropriate, the Deutschmark had been temporarily revalued to allow it to deal with the problems associated with reunification without imposing an unnecessary recession on the other ERM members – would that have produced a superior outcome? I believe that, from the point of view of economic performance, the outcome would not have been as favourable for the UK as was leaving the ERM.

Economic performance after the ERM

After we left the ERM interest rates were cut progressively, to 7 per cent by the end of 1992 and reaching a trough of 5.25 per cent in February 1994. The exchange rate fell below DM2.50. The combination of lower interest rates and a lower exchange rate allowed an economic recovery which gained pace in 1993 and 1994, despite the severe fiscal tightening introduced from late 1992 onwards. Unemployment rose to a little under 3 million at the end of 1992 and then started its more or less uninterrupted fall to today's level (using the claimant count measure) of around 800,000. According to the Treasury's calculations, the output gap, the difference between potential and actual output, was about 4 per cent of GDP in 1993 and was not closed until 1997. That output gap helped to exert downward pressure on inflation at the same time as the economy was growing at an above-trend rate and despite the rise in inflation expectations when we left the ERM. Underlying inflation fell below 3.5 per cent in January 1993 and has stayed in the range 1.5–3.5 per cent ever since. Of course, I am not attempting to attribute all that success to our membership of the ERM – it has been necessary to conduct the right policies since we left – but I do argue that ERM membership provided the foundation for that sustained success.

Was ERM membership necessary?

You may, perhaps, accept that our experience in the ERM caused us to adopt policies that brought down inflation. But it is reasonable to ask whether there was not some other way of achieving the same outcome, but without the political cost (and, indeed, without the cost to the taxpayer of intervention). Why did we have to join the ERM? Why couldn't we have persisted with the policies that preceded it, or have put in place earlier the policies that succeeded it? Here we enter the world of the counter-factual. The best I can hope to do is to offer some convincing arguments.

Could we have continued with the policies that had been put in place before we joined the ERM as an alternative to joining? No doubt we could have done, but my discussion of events leading up to 1990 demonstrates how difficult it had been before ERM entry to choose the correct policies. I have not discussed the political reasons for joining when we did, since they are not relevant to my arguments. They may have been extremely important, but the clear economic reason was to find an alternative and, it was hoped, superior method of conducting a counter-inflationary policy. One way of describing policy-making from around 1972 onwards was that it represented a struggle to learn how to conduct policy in the world of flexible exchange rates. The solution had eluded us, although progress was being made.

There were three peaks of inflation after 1972. The first was at around 30 per cent, the second was at about 20 per cent and the third was at about 10 per cent. We cannot know whether further progress would have been made and, indeed, there is a paradox here to which I shall return shortly. In the circumstances of the time the government did not believe that the experiment should be continued.

In this context I want to return to a point I made earlier. As I have described, interest rates were raised to 15 per cent by the end of 1989 and were held there for a year. That was an essential step in the defeat of inflation. It worked, I believe, because interest rates were held at a high level (though they were cut from their peak) for a further two years after we joined the ERM. Both the initial increases and their maintenance were essential elements in the success of the policy. I cannot rule out the possibility that the same interest rate path would have been followed if we had stayed out of the ERM. The great benefit of ERM membership was that it gave us no choice in the matter.

The conduct of monetary policy after ERM exit

How about the policies that were introduced after we left? It is universally acknowledged that the current framework for monetary policy in the UK is sound and appears enduring. That raises the very reasonable question of whether we needed the ERM experiment at all and could not have moved, in 1990 or earlier, to our present system, or even to the system put in place when we left the ERM in 1992. Nigel Lawson, we know, proposed in 1988 that the Bank of England should be made independent and given the responsibility for preserving the value of the currency (i.e. for maintaining its internal purchasing power).

The decision to set up the Monetary Policy Committee (MPC) after the 1997 general election was brilliant and timely. It demonstrated the government's full commitment to the control of inflation. But it is far from obvious that an earlier move to independence for the Bank of England would have worked, even if it had been politically acceptable. The defeat of inflation requires a political consensus that it is the right thing to do as well as a willingness to pay the temporary cost of achieving it. In a country with our strong tradition of ministerial responsibility and accountability to the House of Commons it is difficult to believe that the problem could have been solved by passing such a responsibility to an independent unelected body. In 1997 the Bank of England was not asked to succeed where politicians had failed; it was asked to maintain the rate of inflation, namely 2.5 per cent, that it inherited. Of course, the MPC has done a brilliant job and its success has far exceeded what might reasonably have been expected, but it was not required to perform miracles.

There is also the question of whether, before 1990, the Bank of England could have solved the technical problems of monetary management that appeared to have defeated the Treasury. And that brings me to the paradox I mentioned earlier. Crudely speaking, we joined the ERM because we could not devise the correct independent monetary policy. We then spent two years without an independent policy. But somehow, when we left the ERM we discovered how to conduct an independent monetary policy. I can recall defending our membership of the ERM during a particularly painful City lunch in the summer of 1992. I remarked that, if we left, our credibility would be completely destroyed. My host replied, 'That depends on what replaces it.' The system that did replace it was set out in Norman Lamont's letter to the chairman of the House of Commons Treasury Committee on 8 October 1992. It worked extraordinarily well. My own view is that the essential elements of success were the establishment of an inflation target and the institution of regular monthly meetings between the Chancellor and the governor to discuss interest rates. The system was further strengthened by the introduction of the Bank of England's Quarterly Inflation Reports and then by the publication of the minutes of the monthly meetings.

Success in designing the post-ERM system cannot be attributed to our experience in the ERM, since, while we were members, our task was simply to keep the exchange rate within its permitted range. Credit must be given to those, principally Norman Lamont, who designed and implemented it.

On the face of it, that system, which allowed the Chancellor to retain the power to set interest rates, could have been introduced much earlier. It particularly raises the question of whether an inflation target could have been introduced earlier. It can be argued, however, that we had tried inflation targets earlier and they had failed. Although the phrase 'inflation target' had not been used, there had of course been policies directed at controlling prices, either as part of prices and incomes policies or as part of more general attempts to control inflation. I can recall discussions of the amount of public expenditure (in the form of subsidies) required to knock a percentage point off the retail price index, for example: a subsidy on coal in summer was particularly good value! That approach, the use of microeconomic instruments to control inflation, was precisely the approach condemned by Nigel Lawson in the Mais Lecture referred to above. It is possible that memories of that type of policy discouraged the introduction of an inflation target; but a more important reason, surely, was that before 1992 the government would not have believed that it had the policy mechanisms that could reliably deliver such a target.

I believe that it is reasonable to argue that the introduction of an inflation target became much more feasible once the steps had been taken to bring inflation down. That was the abiding inheritance of our ERM membership.

Conclusion

A long period of attempts to devise an independent domestic policy to control inflation ended when we joined the ERM in October 1990. The experience of membership was painful and became progressively more so despite cuts in interest rates – real interest rates remained very high. We were members at a time when Germany, a major fellow member of the mechanism, had a particular problem of excess demand. This is a well-recognised potential problem for any currency region. It meant that policies were imposed on other members which generated severe deflation. While we remained a member we were forced to adopt a policy that prolonged a recession. Those extra two years brought inflation down to levels that we have been able to maintain ever since. I do not believe that, in the circumstances of the time, the same effect could have been achieved by other means.

The policies that were put in place after we left, starting with the system introduced in October 1992 and culminating in the establishment of the MPC in 1997, allowed the benefits of ERM membership to be sustained. The economy has also benefited from changes in the supply side and these have contributed to the macroeconomic environment. Those changes, particularly those introduced in the 1980s, have been very much a reflection of the philosophy commemorated by the Wincott Foundation.

The period of membership of the ERM was not a very worthy episode. A slightly cruel summary of it would be to say that we went into the ERM in despair and left in disgrace. Nevertheless, we are still enjoying the benefits of it.

References

Budd, A. (2002), 'The quest for stability', *World Economics*, vol. 3, no. 3, July–September 2002

Budd, A. (2004), *A Tale of Two Economies*, Oxford: the Europaeum

Lawson, N. (1992), *The View from No. 11*, London: Bantam Press

Stephens, P. (1997), *Politics and the Pound: The Tories, the Economy and Europe*, London: Papermac

2 COMMENTARY
Derek Scott[1]

Introduction

Any contribution to a discussion of economic policy from Alan Budd combines intellectual integrity with long practical experience at the highest level, and a generosity of spirit towards others, including politicians.

Budd's case is that, although a political catastrophe (for the Conservative government), and, 'in a sense, an admission of failure', entry to the Exchange Rate Mechanism (ERM) was 'an economic triumph' and marked a turning point in Britain's macroeconomic performance. As he freely acknowledges, however, his thesis depends not only on Britain's brief period of membership of the ERM, but also on leaving it when she did. He concludes that membership of the ERM 'was not a very worthy episode', but argues that 'we are still enjoying the benefits of it'. I discuss this episode in detail in my recent book, *Off Whitehall* (Scott, 2004).

Certainly, since 1992 the performance of the British economy has been remarkable and, as Budd says, one factor has been that, for whatever reason, it became possible to establish a credible monetary framework after the ERM experience in a way that

---

1   Derek Scott is economic consultant to KPMG and was economic adviser to the Prime Minister from 1997 to 2003. He is author of *Off Whitehall*, published by I. B. Tauris in September 2004.

was not possible before; and the Chancellor of the Exchequer at the time of Britain's EU exit, Norman Lamont, is rightly praised for putting this framework together. There is no doubt that this stage of Norman Lamont's career is due for rerating since, in addition to designing a proper framework for monetary policy (later consolidated by Bank of England independence in 1997), he also took most of the tough decisions on spending and tax to put public finances on the road to recovery, although it was Kenneth Clarke's reputation which benefited, and Lamont's policies to bring public finances back into order could only work because monetary policy was set to meet the requirements of the British economy.

At the core of the economic case made by Budd is the argument that the ERM forced the government to maintain policies that brought inflation down to a level where it has (pretty well) stayed ever since. Of course, it was not the ERM itself which brought down inflation, but the level to which UK interest rates were raised within the system: once the medicine had worked, and long before sterling's exit, it was obvious that the interest rates that were imposed through the ERM were inappropriate for Britain. Budd's argument, however, is as much political as economic: without the external discipline of ERM, he argues, politicians would have buckled long before the benefits of the policy to achieve low inflation had been achieved.

This political case for a 'short-term fix' is the most (indeed the only) credible argument for entering the ERM, even if it is made only in hindsight. It is also a much more restricted case for the ERM than most of its proponents put forward at the time or since. Even this political argument for ERM entry, however, is dependent on accepting the political and economic environment as it was in

1990; but could it, and the (necessary) traumas of the ERM, have been avoided?

The results of the mistaken policy of Deutschmark shadowing

Budd refers to Nigel Lawson's attempt to persuade Mrs Thatcher to join the ERM in 1985. He does not say whether he supported the then Chancellor, but describes how, with the ERM option rejected by the Prime Minister, Lawson's policy was for the pound to shadow the Deutschmark. I think Budd may underplay the role of the latter in creating the very conditions that in the end made ERM membership the policy of last resort for the politicians: there was no alternative. Beyond that, however, and perhaps more importantly, although this was no part of the lecture and Budd made clear that nothing in his case for the defence of the ERM could be used to support joining the euro, the lessons of this pre-ERM period (including the aborted attempt to join in 1985) have still not been grasped by advocates of EMU.

For Lawson in 1985 'an historic opportunity had been lost, when the time really had been right'. Others, including Geoffrey Howe and (much later) Tony Blair, shared this view, but it doesn't stand up to serious examination.

In 1985 the British economy was recovering from the 1980/81 recession, but it was a long haul. Between 1980 and 1985 the dollar had been very strong, and at its peak in February 1985 had come close to parity with the pound. In the latter part of 1985 the dollar entered a period of weakness and through the year sterling recovered against all major currencies. Towards the end of 1985 it was a little over DM3.70, the rate at which Nigel Lawson wanted to take sterling into the ERM.

Oil prices declined through the latter part of 1985, but in 1986 the decline turned into a free fall. Lower oil prices helped reduce inflation, but the effect on the British economy was different from that in most other industrialised countries. Lower oil prices raised profits and real incomes: people could spend more, taking up the supply of goods and services that improved profitability made possible. For Britain, as an exporter of oil, the beneficial impact was dented because the fall in oil prices produced a partially offsetting reduction in national income and this lessened the scope for increased domestic spending. So if potential domestic output in the non-oil sector was not to be curtailed it meant diverting external demand to British goods. And the way to do that was through a real depreciation of sterling. This can be effected either through depreciation of the nominal exchange rate or by disinflation, depressing the rate of increase of costs and prices below the rate of increase in other countries. The second option is slow and painful at the best of times, but in 1986 it would have been particularly difficult since inflation in industrial countries was already low and was being further reduced by the fall in oil prices.

Since Britain did not enter the ERM in 1985, sterling continued to float, and between October 1985 and October 1986 the pound fell over 20 per cent against the Deutschmark and 16 per cent in trade-weighted terms. The economy continued growing, but unemployment did not start to fall until October 1986. If sterling had been at a fixed rate within the ERM the real depreciation would still have been necessary, but the alternative route of disinflation would have been forced on the economy. Interest rates would have had to go up dramatically. If policy had aimed to hold sterling at DM3.45, where it was in the middle of 1986, let alone the DM3.70 that Lawson thought was the 'right' exchange rate in November of the previous year, it would have required a sharp rise in UK interest rates, possibly by as much as 7–8 per cent (they remained above 10 per cent for the whole of 1986 as it was). Output and employment would have been crushed. There would have been no recovery.

Of course, subsequently the recovery that did take place got out of hand. But the reason for this was the attempt to prevent a rise in the exchange rate. Lawson's policy of shadowing the Deutschmark was a disaster, particularly in the wake of the favourable supply-side reforms to labour and product markets during the first half of the 1980s. By 1987, the fruits of these reforms were becoming apparent, and the rise in anticipated rates of return was generating a rapid rise in investment expenditure by businesses and households.

When this happens there is a rise in the equilibrium real rate of interest – the rate of interest that keeps the economy in some sort of overall balance. In order for the anticipated real rate of interest in Britain to be above the world rate it is necessary for investors to anticipate a fall in the exchange rate, and for this to happen it must have risen first to levels from which it is expected to decline. The correct response is to raise short-term interest rates and allow the currency to appreciate.

In pursuit of a 'stable' exchange rate Lawson did the opposite. In 1987 sterling was under upward pressure as investors sought the higher rates of return anticipated from sterling assets. The strength of demand in the British economy should have elicited higher interest rates from 1987 onwards. They were edged up in August, but then cut. They were cut first in October 1987 (when there was some justification after the stock market crash, but any cuts in response to that event should have been reversed early) and then again in February and May 1988. These cuts in interest rates were combined with heavy intervention on the foreign exchange markets to curb the rise in sterling. Shortly afterwards, evidence of inflationary pressure became all too obvious. The upshot of trying to keep the pound stable in 1987 and 1988 was an unsustainable inflationary boom. There was a belated decision to uncap the pound in the spring of 1988 but the damage had been done. Inflation was out of control: the rate of increase in the RPI shot up to almost 11 per cent in late 1990.

Inflation at those levels requires draconian monetary tightening and takes a long time to squeeze out of the economy, so that, although the demand boom had already peaked by autumn 1989, it was impossible to start easing monetary policy by cutting interest rates and allowing sterling to start drifting down. On the contrary, as both international investors and domestic businesses and households lost confidence, interest rates were raised in an attempt to restore 'credibility' and get to grips with inflation. Interest rates peaked at 15 per cent in October 1989, where they remained for a year. The initial failure to allow sterling to appreciate meant that the subsequent inflationary surge could be brought under control only by recession.

Fiscal policy not to blame for the boom

Some people put the blame for the boom on purported errors of fiscal policy, in particular the tax-cutting Budgets of 1987 and 1988. It probably was not very sensible to cut taxes at this time, but there was no inherent reason why this relaxation of fiscal policy should lead to the boom and thus to the bust in the way it happened. The boom occurred because of the decision to 'cap' sterling. This stopped monetary policy operating properly and, in particular, prevented the exchange rate from functioning in the way that it should have done and which would have offset fiscal policy 'mistakes'. Furthermore, if monetary policy and the exchange rate had been allowed to work – so avoiding boom and bust – it is likely that the tax cuts would have been shown not to have been an error.

Those who point the finger at fiscal expansion of the late 1980s miss the point. The fiscal expansion did increase demand, but capping the exchange rate meant that there was no mechanism by which either to shift some of that demand to external markets or to help add to the potential supply of the British economy. In those circumstances, of course domestic demand caused a major domestic inflation problem, but the error was one of monetary policy.

Did sterling enter the ERM at the 'wrong' rate?

Many commentators suggest that the rate at which sterling entered in October 1990 was the real cause of subsequent problems within the ERM and an explanation for sterling's exit a couple of years later, the implication being that the pound should have entered at a lower level than the central rate of DM2.95. They point to the fact that the level was decided without consultation with other member states and that the Bundesbank thought the rate too high. Both are true but beside the point.

In 1985 Nigel Lawson wanted to take sterling into the ERM at a central rate of DM3.70. In his memoirs he says that the fall in oil prices the following year would have justified a realignment of the pound. He suggests that sterling would have participated in the general realignment that took place within the ERM in April 1986, moving to something closer to DM3.50. This retrospective view exposes some important issues that have to be addressed by anyone thinking of supporting entry to EMU. First, Lawson, who was against EMU but who certainly believed in the disciplines of the ERM, could not possibly have anticipated the opportunity or the need for the pound to depreciate if he had been successful in taking it into the ERM at DM3.70.

Second, the reasons for the necessary depreciation that Lawson identified were not brought about by any policy failing in Britain, but by changes in the international economy that affected this country differently from others. It is very doubtful in practice whether sterling would have been allowed to devalue within months of entering the ERM. But in any case realignments within the system were not made in response to genuine changes in economic circumstances. Within the ERM realignments were permitted only to restore 'competitiveness'. In EMU necessary realignments, whether on grounds of 'competitiveness' or changed circumstances, are impossible.

Third, even had sterling been in the ERM and devalued in 1986, it would have been necessary shortly afterwards to revalue the pound because of the rise in rates of return and the incipient investment boom that were induced by the supply-side reforms of the 1980s. Again, in practice, this would not have been possible in the ERM, since no currency was permitted to revalue against the Deutschmark. More importantly in the context of EMU, neither the depreciation nor the appreciation would have been possible, but the need for both illustrates how swiftly the appropriate level for a currency can alter.

The lesson for EMU

In his memoirs Lawson says:

> I could not help noticing that that those who castigated John
> Major for having joined at an excessively high rate of DM
> 2.95 to the pound were the same as those who had earlier
> castigated me for having shadowed the Deutschmark at the
> excessively low rate of DM 3.00 to the pound … there is no
> way that it can seriously be maintained both that DM 3.00
> was too low in 1988 and DM 2.95 significantly too high in
> 1990.

What this fails to recognise, and what those who are preoccupied with the exchange rate at which sterling should enter EMU fail to recognise, is that it is the very fact that the appropriate real exchange rate can move very significantly which causes economic difficulties within fixed exchange rate systems. Within such systems, the only way the real exchange rate can adjust is through relative inflation and deflation. The alternative of the real exchange rate adjusting through movements in the nominal exchange rate is no longer available. There is no permanently correct exchange rate for the currency even if, at the moment of entry, the rate is in some sense 'right'. Today, the countries in the euro zone are coming to realise that they may have gained nominal currency stability with each other, but only at the cost of greater instability in the things that matter: output and jobs.

References

Scott, D. (2004), *Off Whitehall: A View from Downing Street by Tony Blair's Adviser*, London: I. B. Tauris

3 COMMENTARY
Tim Congdon[1]

The origins of the ERM

Sir Alan Budd's Wincott Lecture tries to justify UK macro-economic policy during the late 1980s and early 1990s. In particular, he commends the UK's membership of the European Exchange Rate Mechanism (ERM) between 6 October 1990, when the British government announced that the pound would participate, and 16 September 1992, when it was expelled by heavy selling on the foreign exchanges. But the story really begins in 1972. On 1 May 1972 the British government had decided to join the European 'snake', an exchange rate agreement (under the auspices of the European Economic Community) that was the forerunner of the ERM. From the start the snake was, to all intents and purposes, led by West Germany's central bank, the Bundesbank. On 26 June – after a mere eight weeks – the UK left the snake and floated the pound, having lost $2.5 billion of foreign exchange reserves in six days.

The context of the pound's misfortunes in the summer of 1972 was the realisation by European countries that the Bretton Woods system of fixed exchange rates had broken down. In the heyday of that system (i.e. in the 1950s and early 1960s) the US managed

---

1   Professor Tim Congdon is Chief Economist at Lombard Street Research and served on the Treasury's Panel of Independent Forecasters established in the wake of Britain's exit from the ERM.

its own currency in a sound, anti-inflationary way, virtually all the world's currencies were tied to the US dollar and, because of the exchange rate link, the world as a whole enjoyed the benefits of low American inflation. But between the mid-1960s and the early 1980s US monetary policy was irresponsible and inflationary. West Germany – a nation scarred by its memories of the Weimar hyper-inflation of the 1920s – wanted to avoid the contamination of domestic monetary policy by US mistakes. Ever since its foundation in 1957 the Bundesbank had believed in a monetary theory of inflation (i.e. that inflation is caused by excessive growth of the quantity of money relative to the growth of output). In the five years to end-1972 the US money supply (on the M3 measure) grew at a compound annual rate of 9.7 per cent. If the German currency – the Deutschmark – had stayed pegged to the US dollar while the US money supply was growing at this sort of rate, West Germany could not have avoided significant inflation. In May 1971 the German government broke the link with the dollar and let the Deutschmark float upwards on the foreign exchange markets.

Over the next few months West Germany and its EEC partners tried to assemble a European fixed exchange rate system. On 7 March 1972 EEC finance ministers decided to form the snake, in which the participant European currencies could fluctuate relative to each other within a narrow 2.25 per cent band. This was the beginning of the process of European monetary integration which was to culminate in the introduction of the euro on 1 January 1999. Throughout the following 27 years West Germany – with its voice at international gatherings often being indistinguishable from the Bundesbank's – was the key nation promoting monetary integration. The attitude of other European nations varied widely. The Netherlands joined forces with West Germany from the outset and never wavered. In the mid- and late 1970s West Germany, the Netherlands, Austria and Switzerland formed an island of financial stability in a mismanaged and highly inflationary world. The UK was equivocal about European monetary integration in 1972 and remains so to this day.

British economists' opposition to the monetary theory of inflation

Intellectual trends in the economics profession of the English-speaking nations – and particularly in Britain itself – had been hostile to the monetary theory of inflation since the publication of Keynes's *The General Theory of Employment, Interest and Money* in 1936. But the lesson of West Germany's success in the 1970s was not lost on the British political class, even if it was beyond a surprisingly high proportion of British economists. UK inflation, as measured by the annual change in the retail price index, peaked in August 1975 at 26.9 per cent. Money supply targets – expressed in terms of broad money – were introduced in July 1976. With long-term intellectual impetus from Enoch Powell and Keith Joseph, the Conservative Party accepted the monetary theory of inflation. After her success in the 1979 general election the leader of the Conservative Party, Mrs Thatcher, made clear that her government would reduce inflation by controlling the money supply, not by means of administered price and wage controls.

So outraged was the British economics profession by Thatcher's monetary (or 'monetarist') approach that the government had considerable difficulty finding academic sympathisers who would advise it on its favoured course of action. Fortunately, economists at the London Business School – notably James Ball, Terence Burns and Alan Budd – had written papers in the mid- and late 1970s on monetary topics, and were regarded as generally in favour of monetarism. Burns was appointed the government's Chief Economic Adviser in 1979 at the young age of 35. Burns or Budd (or sometimes Burns and Budd) occupied important positions in the economic policy-making machine for the next 20 years. Burns was the driving force within the official machine behind the introduction of the Medium Term Financial Strategy (MTFS) in March 1980. This strategy specified targets for the budget deficit and money supply growth for the next four years.

As Budd says, the early 1980s were a difficult period in the implementation of the agenda of monetary control. Financial liberalisation and the abolition of exchange controls were contemporaneous with a step-shift in the level of real interest rates, from negative values in the 1970s to positive values in the 1980s. The result was an abrupt change in the trend of the equilibrium ratio of money to income. Whereas this ratio had been falling for over thirty years until the late 1970s, it was on a rising trend thereafter. Budd is correct in saying that this change of trend weakened the credibility of the money supply targets set out in the 1980 version of the MTFS, because these were patently too low. An unexpectedly large once-for-all adjustment to the sterling M3 money measure in the summer of 1980, following the scrapping of the 'corset', was a particularly serious presentational problem.[2]

However, the government insisted – correctly – that low inflation could be restored only by reductions in money supply growth. Considerable political courage was shown by Sir Geoffrey Howe in

---

2   The 'corset' was a quantified limit on banks' eligible liabilities. These liabilities included bank deposits, which were the dominant part of sterling M3.

adhering to the essence of the MTFS while he remained Chancellor of the Exchequer. The annual rate of broad money growth (on the sterling M3 measure), which had often been in the high teens or even the twenties in the 1970s, was just above 10 per cent in the years to end-1983 and end-1984. Because of the rise in the desired ratio of money to incomes, these numbers were consistent with 5 per cent inflation.

Policy mistakes in the mid-1980s

By 1985 money supply targets had been in existence for almost a decade and had achieved a signal improvement in the UK's macroeconomic circumstances. Inflation was somewhat higher than in West Germany and the Netherlands, but it was lower than in France or Italy. Despite all the brickbats hurled at monetarism in the early 1980s, domestic monetary control had worked. The UK had reduced annual inflation from numbers well above 20 per cent to an internationally respectable 5 per cent, and it had done so while remaining outside the European snake and the European Monetary System (which succeeded the snake in 1979). The Conservatives' original agenda could have been retained in the late 1980s, with further reductions in money supply growth and the eventual establishment of price stability.

But this was not what the Thatcher government did. Instead, Nigel Lawson – who had succeeded Howe as Chancellor in 1983 – committed a U-turn in monetary policy. He suspended targets for the growth of broad money in October 1985, as the prelude to scrapping them in 1986. Money supply growth accelerated in late 1985 and 1986, and by the end of 1986 the annual rate of increase in the sterling M3 measure had soared to 18 per cent. It continued to run at this sort of rate until 1989. The result of the abandonment of domestic monetary control was predictable and predicted.[3] Marked asset price inflation developed in 1986 and 1987, and was accompanied by a sharp upturn in the growth of domestic demand. Output boomed, unemployment fell and the current account of the balance of payments lurched heavily into the red. By late 1989 – when Lawson resigned – inflation was plainly on the rise. The annual rate of increase in the retail price index was to peak at over 10 per cent one year later.

One mistake compounded by another

It was the catastrophic failure on inflation which led to the decision by Lawson's successor, John Major, to join the ERM in November 1990. As Budd says, the Treasury and the Bank of England had decided that the job of conducting British monetary policy was too difficult for them, and that they ought to give it to the Bundesbank. By this stage the ERM was far more meaningful than the original snake. France, Belgium and Luxembourg had made almost as emphatic a commitment to exchange rate stability

---

3   See Congdon (1992), which gives a selection of his articles in *The Times* from 1985 to 1988, where he warned of the likely consequences of rapid money supply growth. His newspaper articles borrowed from themes of his work at the stock-brokers L. Messel & Co. In a Messel research note of 18 October 1985, 'Sterling M3 is not meaningless', written only a few days after Lawson's suspension of the broad money target, he wrote, 'In the early stages of both the Barber boom and the Healey boomlet [which had seen rising money growth, followed by higher inflation], excess sterling M3 growth was accompanied by low inflation. It took two or three years before the full inflationary damage came through. Inflation may drop in 1986 [it did], but that does not allow Mr. Lawson to claim that he is innocent to the charge of monetary mismanagement. A better verdict would be "not yet proven guilty, while awaiting trial".' (The research note is available from the author at tim.congdon@lombardstreetresearch.com.)

within Europe, and to eventual European monetary integration, as the Netherlands had at the outset. Meanwhile the Bundesbank had adhered to money supply targets – expressed in terms of the broad M3 measure – for over fifteen years and maintained its reputation for inflation control.

But – very plainly – the UK did *not* have to join the ERM in order to combat double-digit inflation. To repeat, the UK had between 1976 and 1985 reduced inflation from over 20 per cent to 5 per cent by domestic monetary control. As in West Germany, the centrepiece of the UK's system had been money targets expressed in terms of a broad measure of money. Despite many technical embarrassments, that system worked.[4] Contrary to Budd's claim that the UK needed 'a nominal anchor' in the form of a fixed exchange rate, the UK's experience in the period from 1972 to 1985 had demonstrated two unsurprising points. The first point was that inflation is caused by faster growth in the quantity of money than that in goods and services, and the second was that control over the

4   It is even possible that by 1989 Lawson came to realise that his U-turn on money supply targets had been a blunder, even though he denies this in his account of his years as Chancellor of the Exchequer in Lawson (1992). Lawson's final Mansion House speech, in October 1989, included a detailed discussion of broad money and funding policy. The extent of his comments was such that he evidently continued to worry about the subject, even if he remained critical of the pre-1985 system of monetary control. In an article in the *Financial Times* on 23 October, Samuel Brittan said that the days of 'old M3' were 'still immensely better than what is normally said on such occasions'. (This statement was curiously out of character. Brittan has been highly critical of money supply targets as 'monetarist mumbo-jumbo' over the last 20 years.) On 26 October Lawson resigned, ostensibly in protest against Sir Alan Walters's influence on the Prime Minister's views on economic policy. In an article on Lawson's resignation on 27 October Brittan remarked that the fiscal side of the medium-term financial strategy was 'very much alive and the monetary side will be taken up again'. It is well known that Lawson and Brittan conferred frequently in this period.

quantity of money is necessary and sufficient for a reduction in inflation. The right step in 1989 was to reintroduce an effective system of domestic monetary restraint, perhaps buttressed by granting independence to the Bank of England. The lesson of history – in West Germany, the UK and many other countries – was that broad money targets constituted such a system.[5]

Monetary growth is the best predictor of inflation

It was the blunder in ending broad money targets in 1985 and the subsequent explosion in money supply growth which were responsible for the Lawson boom. Budd asserts, 'Money supply targets were unsatisfactory because it was extremely difficult, if not impossible, to establish stable demand functions for money.' This statement is politely described as an evasion in search of a half-truth. The supposed absence (or disappearance) of a stable money demand function would indeed have had a message for the conduct of macroeconomic policy, but words need to be used with care when econometric results are translated into policy prescriptions.

When a statistical relationship is estimated between, say, the rate of change in nominal national income (as the dependent or 'y' variable) and the rate of change in a money aggregate (as the independent or 'x' variable), it has a number of properties represented by the values of the regression coefficient, the correlation coefficient, the standard error of the equation, the so-called 't'-statistics indicating the statistical significance of the regression coefficient (or coefficients), and so on. Suppose that the money–GDP rela-

---

5   The argument was made in Congdon (1989).

tionship was less stable in the 1980s than in the 1970s. The meaning of the decline in stability is that – because the correlation coefficient was lower and the standard error higher with the 1980s equation than with the 1970s equation – a policy-maker in the later decade can forecast *with less confidence* the central value of the rate of increase in nominal GDP associated with a particular rate of increase in money.[6]

This would be a disappointment for a supporter of money supply targets, but it would not be the end of the world. *A change in the degree of confidence* with which a forecast is delivered must not be confused with *a change in the central value of the dependent variable(s) implied by particular values of the independent variable(s)*. Even after the supposed deterioration in the stability of the money–income relationships in the early 1980s, it was still essential for policy-makers to know *the most likely value* of the increase in nominal GDP that would follow a particular rate of money supply growth. That depended on the regression coefficient, not the correlation coefficient or the standard error. As long as the regression coefficient on an estimated money–GDP relationship was significantly positive, it remained true in 1985 (as it was in 1975, or indeed 1875 or 2005) that *the most likely outcome of an acceleration in money supply growth would be an acceleration in the growth rate of nominal GDP and, in due course, of inflation.*

Money and inflation in the mid- to late 1980s

Budd has three problems here. The first is that the alleged instability of the demand function for broad money was not new in

---

6   Strictly, the probability statements apply to a band of values either side of the most likely central value.

the mid-1980s. Research at the Bank of England and elsewhere had usually found stable demand functions for broad money in the 1960s, but two papers were published by Artis and Lewis in 1974 and 1976 arguing that these functions had broken down.[7] The breakdown was evidenced in lower values of correlation coefficients and higher values of standard errors, but (as far as the author is aware) a routine finding in all the 1970s work remained that the regression coefficients in money–GDP relationships were significantly positive. The relatively poor correlation coefficients and standard errors in the broad money equations had a clear policy implication, but – contrary to Budd's claim – this was not that the whole machinery of money supply targets should be dumped. Because it was unrealistic to expect a reliable y per cent nominal GDP response to a particular x per cent money growth rate in any one year, control over the money aggregates had to extend over several years. Money targets had to be medium term and pragmatic in nature, as they were in West Germany. That was one reason why supporters of the Conservatives' monetarist agenda advocated a *medium-term* financial strategy.[8]

Budd's second difficulty is that the contrast in the rates of money growth before and after mid-1985 was so large and egre-

---

7   Artis and Lewis (1981: 17). In fact the difficulties with money demand functions in the UK were not new even in the mid-1970s. One of the earliest studies of money and the business cycle in the UK was by Walters (1966). Walters noted that money had a good relationship with nominal GDP in the 1877–1913 and 1921–38 periods, but his comment on the quarterly data in the 1955–62 period was that they 'fail to demonstrate the existence of a marked systematic relationship between the quantity of money and prices and income'.

8   The advocacy of money supply targets over a medium-term horizon was also influenced by the recommendation of 'gradualism' in monetary restraint made by Professors David Laidler and Michael Parkin at the Manchester Inflation Workshop in the mid-1970s.

gious that any statistical difficulties in the money–income relationship were incidental. But, whereas sterling M3 rose at an annual rate of 10.3 per cent in the three years to mid-1985, it climbed at an annual rate of 19.4 per cent in the three years to mid-1988! Bluntly, it is astonishing that the Treasury and the Bank of England did not foresee what would happen to the economy in general terms, even if no forecaster could be confident (to a level of statistical significance arbitrarily determined by an econometric boffin) of a decimal-point forecast of nominal GDP, inflation, consumption and so on.

The third point is that it is far from clear that the demand for money in the UK did become unstable in the 1980s. The change in the trend of the money–income ratio cannot be disputed, and it was undoubtedly a major embarrassment for the government and supporters of money supply targets. But a change in the equilibrium money–income ratio could be attributable to changes in the values of the determinants of the quantity of money demanded rather than to large changes in the properties (the regression and correlation coefficients, and so on) of money demand functions. The author – with the support of teams at L. Messel & Co. in the 1980s and Lombard Street Research in the 1990s – has had no difficulty in identifying a stable demand function for personal sector money throughout the period.[9] Since the personal sector was and remains the largest holder of money balances in the UK economy,

9   See Congdon (2004). The author first reported in May 1986 on the stability of personal sector money demand in a joint L. Messel & Co. research note with Peter Warburton (available at tim.congdon@lombardstreetresearch.com). The stability of the personal sector's money demand function has been corroborated by other researchers and is now widely accepted: see Drake and Chrystal (1997) and Thomas (1997).

this finding goes far to refute Budd's scepticism about money demand functions. Further, the behaviour of the two other components of the private sector – companies and financial institutions – was undoubtedly influenced by their balance-sheet positions (including their money holdings) in the 1980s, as it was in every other decade in modern British history. (Treasury officials may not have to explain themselves to the bank manager, but finance directors and small businessmen don't have that luxury.)

Britain's economic performance since ERM exit

But that is enough on the technicalities. The passage of events since 1992 tells its own tale, without the need to rely on high-powered econometrics. It is surely obvious that the UK's inflation record since 1992 refutes Budd's central contention. The UK has kept inflation down at a moderate figure with remarkably little variation, while eschewing both membership of the ERM and adoption of the euro. If it has been able for over a decade to maintain low inflation without the artificial crutch of a fixed exchange rate, it could have reduced inflation from 1989 to 1992 also without the artificial crutch of a fixed exchange rate. Budd's Wincott Lecture has its attractive side, with its wit and humour about mistakes in high places. But in its failure to acknowledge the main lesson from over twenty years of policy-making, it is misguided. The pound was kicked out of the snake on 26 June 1972 in humiliating circumstances, because earlier mismanagement of domestic monetary policy had made the exchange rate untenable; and it was again kicked out of the ERM on 16 September 1992 in humiliating circumstances, because earlier mismanagement of domestic monetary policy had made the exchange rate untenable.

The imperative – in 1972, in 1992 and in all the years in between – was to manage domestic monetary policy properly.

As Germany showed by its pursuit of money supply targets throughout this period, a consistent, intellectually coherent and self-confident approach to policy-making would deliver results. The Lawson boom and the two years of bust in the ERM were episodes of shocking incompetence. If the UK had persevered with a steady reduction in money supply growth from 1985 onwards, it could have enjoyed stable growth with falling inflation in the late 1980s and early 1990s. It could have avoided the disastrous boom-bust cycle for which Budd is much too ready to find a face-saving explanation.

References

Artis, M. J. and M. K. Lewis (1981), *Monetary Control in the United Kingdom*, Oxford: Philip Allan

Congdon, T. (1989), *Monetarism Lost*, London: Centre for Policy Studies

Congdon, T. (1992), *Reflections on Monetarism*, Aldershot: Edward Elgar

Congdon, T. (2004), 'Monetarism: a rejoinder', *World Economics*, 5(3): 179–97

Drake, L. and K. A. Chrystal (1997), 'Personal sector money demand in the UK', *Oxford Economic Papers*, 49(2): 188–206

Lawson, N. (1992), *The View from No. 11*, London: Bantam Press

Thomas, R. S. J. (1997), 'The demand for M4: a sectoral analysis. Part I – the personal sector', Working Paper no. 61, London: Bank of England

Walters, A. A. (1966), 'Monetary multipliers in the UK 1880–1962', *Oxford Economic Papers*, 18(3): 270–83

4 COMMENTARY

Samuel Brittan[1]

Norman Lamont once remarked that membership of the Exchange Rate Mechanism (ERM) in 1990–92 was beneficial in bringing down rapidly the British inflation rate but that exit from the system was also beneficial in promoting recovery from recession. This is more or less the line taken by Sir Alan Budd now; and I agree with them.

What I would like to do in this commentary is to say a little about the European and British political background and then go on to a few implications of Sir Alan Budd's analysis. A common fault among both proponents and opponents of ERM membership was to see the system purely in terms of the British debate and not to examine how the ERM participants – the core members of the EU – themselves saw it.

The exchange rate anchor

'Fixed but adjustable' exchange rates prevailed under the Bretton Woods system after World War II, with the emphasis shifting to 'reluctant adjustment'. They were seen as a way of bringing order

---

1   Sir Samuel Brittan is a columnist at the *Financial Times*. His most recent books are *Against the Flow: Reflections of an Individualist* (Atlantic Books, 2005) and *Essays, Moral, Political and Economic* (Edinburgh University Press, 1998).

into international monetary relationships without the straitjacket of the old gold standard.

The system worked with the dollar as the 'anchor currency' against which other currencies were fixed. In the European ERM the Deutschmark became the anchor for member countries. By the 1980s many economists and commentators had begun to see such systems as a back-door method of achieving and maintaining low inflation. The idea was that if a country had a stable exchange rate against a low-inflation country it could in a sense 'borrow' that country's credibility. It was even sometimes described as 'monetarism by the back door'.

A Deutschmark anchor was, however, far from the intention of the founding fathers of the system, which arose as a result of the initiative of the French and German leaders Valéry Giscard d'Estaing and Helmut Schmidt in the late 1970s (in the wake of earlier prodding by Roy Jenkins during his period as president of the Commission). A large part of their objective was to combat the domination of the dollar. To the extent that they worked it out, what they meant by this was the ability of the US to absorb resources from the rest of the world by running a large balance of payments deficit financed by other countries accumulating dollar assets.[2]

The ERM became a Deutschmark anchor system largely as a result of the actions of the Bundesbank, which continued to operate German monetary policy in what it regarded as German interests. For a large part of the 1980s French interest rates could be above German ones because of the risks of downward realignment. This

---

2   Twenty-five years later, with European Monetary Union up and running, the US is doing exactly the same on a larger scale.

was the system that most of the advocates of British membership – apart from the out-and-out European federalists – wished to join and which Margaret Thatcher and Alan Walters so vehemently opposed.

But, even as the battle lines were being drawn up in the UK, the Europeans had, as so often, moved the goalposts. Realising that the ERM had not worked out as intended they set up the Delors Committee to work out plans for a genuine monetary union. That committee seized the bull by the horns and declared that it would mean a single currency. After the committee reported in 1989, the aim was to make realignments of the ERM small and rare to provide a glide path to monetary union. By the time the British had plucked up their courage and embraced membership in 1990 the ERM was transforming itself into something very different.

In 1993 the Delors plan threatened to blow apart in a wave of currency storms (following the 1992 wave which had forced the UK outside). But European finance ministers decided that, rather than abandoning the ERM altogether, they should widen the margins of fluctuation to 15 per cent each way. The characteristic British reaction was to regard this as just a fig leaf. Kenneth Clarke (who ironically was the originator of the 15 per cent suggestion) had no intention of fighting a domestic political battle to return to what had then become an extremely unpopular system. But, as so often in the past, the core EU members took commitments and timetables seriously and eventually reduced to a very small margin currency fluctuations against the Deutschmark, leading to the formal establishment of EMU in 1999 and the domestic circulation of euros in 2002.

COMMENTARY BY SAMUEL BRITTAN

British political implications

The ERM has had a longer history in British domestic politics than generally realised. Well before the 1979 election, when Labour was still in power, a Treasury official gave a strongly worded but unattributable briefing criticising the ERM and saying why it was not in British interests to join. The Prime Minister, James Callaghan, had apparently decided from the beginning that the Labour Party would not countenance British membership. At the time Labour was more sceptical of the EU than the Conservatives, and the currency project appeared to those who thought about it at all as a bankers' ramp to impose deflation on the UK.

Nigel Lawson makes it very clear in his memoirs[3] that his initial impetus to join the ERM came from observing that the very same ministers – the so-called 'wets' – who were most opposed to domestic counter-inflationary stringency were also enthusiastic supporters of projects associated with the European Union. This element persisted right through to the end in that notorious 1992 ministerial meeting when exit from the ERM was delayed by a crucial few hours and the reserve losses mounted, while pro-European ministers fought against the odds to save British membership.

It is impossible to overestimate the political fallout from the forced departure from the ERM. Although few voters would have remembered the precise details, it destroyed the Conservative reputation for economic competence. The repercussions extended to the Labour Party as well. The former Labour leader John Smith was an enthusiast for the ERM, precisely because he believed that it provided an alternative to the party's previous painful attempts to obtain pay restraint from the unions directly. Gordon Brown

3   Lawson (1993).

was Labour's economic spokesman at the time; and it was in the post-ERM period that Tony Blair moved ahead of him in the party popularity stakes. Of course, there were larger elements involved; but the ERM episode helped give a jolt to the comparative reputations of the two men at a crucial moment.

The key British error

Could the UK have stayed in the ERM? I believe many mistakes were made in defence of the ERM parity (some of them are detailed in Stephens, 1997, and Lawson, 1993) but the one I felt most strongly about was the surprise expressed by the British authorities at the size of the speculative movement against the pound. If there is one lesson to be learned from attempts to defend parities, it is that the movement of speculative funds is likely to be many times greater than anything to be expected based on previous experience.

But I do not want to dwell on this aspect here. A more successful defence would have meant higher interest rates for longer. Even if the British government had been prepared to entertain this, the markets would not have believed that it would have stayed the course in the face of soaring unemployment and falling output.

The big error surrounding the eventual entry into the ERM in 1990 concerned European politics. From the time that the Berlin Wall fell in November 1989 and German unity loomed, the Deutschmark was no longer suitable as an anchor currency. That should certainly have been apparent by October 1990 when the UK joined. Unfortunately nearly all the politicians, officials and commentators who had previously urged ERM membership continued to do so despite the way in which German unification was being handled: and I include myself. Our minds operated on two tracks: cheering on German political reunification, while continuing to view British problems in our usual insular way.

After membership

Alan Budd is quite right to say that experience in the ERM brought inflation down with a rapidity and to a level that would have been extremely difficult to achieve by domestic means. In the highbrow literature there is, I believe, an expression known as 'opportunistic disinflation'. This means that the authorities in high-inflation countries will not deliberately impose a sufficiently fierce domestic squeeze to bring inflation down from, say, double digits to 2 or 3 per cent. But they will take advantage of any outside events to – as Gordon Brown might put it – 'lock in' the lower rate of inflation thus achieved. Could disinflation in Britain have been achieved more slowly and less painfully without the 1990–92 episode? There is a sporting chance that it might have been if the first attempt at membership had not been vetoed by Margaret Thatcher, in November 1985, when German unification was still a distant dream. The model that many ERM supporters then had in mind was France. That country was prepared to make downward realignments within the ERM but reluctantly, treating it as a sort of mini Bretton Woods. For such a policy to have had a chance of success in Britain, sterling would have had to realign with the franc in 1986 (as Lawson concedes in his memoirs) without undermining policy credibility. Whether that would have been possible, given the hysteria that has so often surrounded discussion of the exchange rate in Britain, I do not know.

How the inflation target was prepared

One favourable surprise after Black Wednesday was the speed with which an alternative policy was put together. Nearly all the key characteristics of the present – and so far successful – stable monetary regime were announced within a few weeks of the exit from the ERM. These included the inflation target; the Bank of England's quarterly inflation report; the formal monthly meetings, followed, when Kenneth Clarke became Chancellor in 1993, by publication of the minutes of these meetings. These paved the way for operational independence for the Bank and the establishment of the Monetary Policy Committee. Many of these policies were first contained in embryonic form in a letter dated 8 October 1992, from Norman Lamont to the Conservative chairman of the House of Commons Treasury Committee. They apparently emerged from a meeting between the Prime Minister, the Chancellor and senior Treasury officials in Brighton, on the fringes of the Conservative party conference (Stephens, 1997: 266–7). It is difficult, however, to see how such a comprehensive framework could have emerged so quickly after Black Wednesday unless at least a few people had been thinking about policy in a non-ERM world well before the UK was forced to leave. I am reminded of the period up to the 1967 sterling devaluation when the subject was treated as 'the great unmentionable', but a few people had obviously thought about it to be prepared for the day when it happened.

One question raised by Alan Budd is whether Britain as a country could have adopted an inflation target earlier. He quotes Peter Middleton as saying that there was some kind of inflation target several years before. But that target belonged to a different era when incomes policy was still seen as the main way of tackling inflation and the target was set in that context. It was both a guiding light for pay settlements and held out – rather dangerously – as a reward for the unions if they stuck with the policy. Inflation targets, in relation to a monetary approach to inflation, were hardly known until about 1990 when New Zealand was the first country to experiment with them. And I must admit that if I had been asked at any time in the 1980s about such a target I would have said: 'How do you enforce it? You are describing only the goal and not the means.' Even if it had been advocated in conjunction with an independent Bank of England, I would still have asked: 'How does the Bank go about it?'

EMU lessons

I would like to elaborate on why the ERM episode holds almost no lessons for the desirability or otherwise of Britain joining the euro. This is because, despite superficial similarities, they are two entirely different systems. The ERM was an exchange rate system rather like Bretton Woods; and monetary discipline came from the exchange rate constraint. There is no such constraint within the European Monetary Union for the very simple reason that there are no exchange rates between the euro countries. Their separate currencies have been abolished (and there has been rightly no attempt to use the euro–dollar rate or the euro–yen rate as a counter-inflationary constraint). The euro system is in fact very similar to the present British system with an independent central bank and a low inflation target.

Leaving aside the rather political emotions on either side, the economic question is whether we would do better to have this system operated by the Bank of England's Monetary Policy Committee (MPC) or by the European Central Bank (ECB). It is a question of trading off the advantages of ending exchange rate fluctuations against countries accounting for a good half of our overseas trade against the disadvantages of a one-size-fits-all monetary policy adapted to average conditions in the euro area rather than those in any particular country. Until a couple of years ago I would have said that it was six of one and half a dozen of the other. But today I would be more inclined to say it is seven in favour of the MPC system and only five in favour of joining the ECB.

Adjustable pegs

There is a final and more general question. The almost universal fashion today is to believe that a country must make a choice between a floating exchange rate and merging its currency with that of a wider area. Even the halfway house of a currency board has been out of favour since the Argentinian collapse. Economic fashions change rapidly and unpredictably. Even so, I do not see an early return to Bretton Woods-type systems or even G7-type currency range targets. Such a shift could come about, of course, if globalisation were to collapse and we went back to tight exchange control and restricted capital movements, which would be technically very difficult – but not impossible in the face of strong populist political reaction. In that case far more would be at stake than the currency regime.

References

Lawson, N. (1993), *The View from No. 11*, London: Bantam Press
Stephens, P. (1997), *Politics and the Pound: The Tories, the Economy and Europe*, London: Papermac

ABOUT THE IEA

The Institute is a research and educational charity (No. CC 235 351), limited by guarantee. Its mission is to improve understanding of the fundamental institutions of a free society with particular reference to the role of markets in solving economic and social problems.

The IEA achieves its mission by:

- a high-quality publishing programme
- conferences, seminars, lectures and other events
- outreach to school and college students
- brokering media introductions and appearances

The IEA, which was established in 1955 by the late Sir Antony Fisher, is an educational charity, not a political organisation. It is independent of any political party or group and does not carry on activities intended to affect support for any political party or candidate in any election or referendum, or at any other time. It is financed by sales of publications, conference fees and voluntary donations.

In addition to its main series of publications the IEA also publishes a quarterly journal, *Economic Affairs*, and has two specialist programmes – Environment and Technology, and Education.

The IEA is aided in its work by a distinguished international Academic Advisory Council and an eminent panel of Honorary Fellows. Together with other academics, they review prospective IEA publications, their comments being passed on anonymously to authors. All IEA papers are therefore subject to the same rigorous independent refereeing process as used by leading academic journals.

IEA publications enjoy widespread classroom use and course adoptions in schools and universities. They are also sold throughout the world and often translated/reprinted.

Since 1974 the IEA has helped to create a world-wide network of 100 similar institutions in over 70 countries. They are all independent but share the IEA's mission.

Views expressed in the IEA's publications are those of the authors, not those of the Institute (which has no corporate view), its Managing Trustees, Academic Advisory Council members or senior staff.

Members of the Institute's Academic Advisory Council, Honorary Fellows, Trustees and Staff are listed on the following page.

The Institute gratefully acknowledges financial support for its publications programme and other work from a generous benefaction by the late Alec and Beryl Warren.

THE WINCOTT MEMORIAL LECTURES

1 **The Counter-Revolution in Monetary Theory**
MILTON FRIEDMAN
1970 *Occasional Paper 33* 5th Impression 1983 £1.00

2 **Wages and Prices in a Mixed Economy**
JAMES E. MEADE
1971 *Occasional Paper 35* Out of print

3 **Government and High Technology**
JOHN JEWKES
1972 *Occasional Paper 37* Out of print

4 **Economic Freedom and Representative Government**
F. A. HAYEK
1973 *Occasional Paper 39* 3rd Impression 1980 Out of print

5 **Aspects of Post-war Economic Policy**
LORD ROBBINS
1974 *Occasional Paper 42* £1.00

19 **1992: Europe's Last Chance?**
From Common Market to Single Market
VICTORIA CURZON PRICE
1988 *Occasional Paper 81* £5.00

20 **The Limits of International Co-operation**
DEEPAK LAL
1990 *Occasional Paper 83* £4.00

22 **Do Currency Boards Have a Future?**
ANNA J. SCHWARTZ
1992 *Occasional Paper 88* £2.95

23 **Finance – Villain or Scapegoat?**
HAROLD ROSE
1994 *Occasional Paper 92* £3.50

24 **Free Trade, 'Fairness' and the New Protectionism**
Reflections on an Agenda for the World Trade Organisation
JAGDISH BHAGWATI
1995 *Occasional Paper 96* £4.00

25 **Competition Regulation the British Way:
Jaguar or Dinosaur?**
SIR BRYAN CARSBERG
1996 *Occasional Paper 97* £4.00

Other papers recently published by the IEA include:

WHO, What and Why?

Transnational Government, Legitimacy and the World Health Organization
Roger Scruton
Occasional Paper 113; ISBN 0 255 36487 3
£8.00

The World Turned Rightside Up

A New Trading Agenda for the Age of Globalisation
John C. Hulsman
Occasional Paper 114; ISBN 0 255 36495 4
£8.00

The Representation of Business in English Literature

Introduced and edited by Arthur Pollard
Readings 53; ISBN 0 255 36491 1
£12.00

Anti-Liberalism 2000

The Rise of New Millennium Collectivism
David Henderson
Occasional Paper 115; ISBN 0 255 36497 0
£7.50

Capitalism, Morality and Markets

Brian Griffiths, Robert A. Sirico, Norman Barry & Frank Field
Readings 54; ISBN 0 255 36496 2
£7.50

A Conversation with Harris and Seldon

Ralph Harris & Arthur Seldon
Occasional Paper 116; ISBN 0 255 36498 9
£7.50

Malaria and the DDT Story

Richard Tren & Roger Bate
Occasional Paper 117; ISBN 0 255 36499 7
£10.00

A Plea to Economists Who Favour Liberty: Assist the Everyman

Daniel B. Klein
Occasional Paper 118; ISBN 0 255 36501 2
£10.00

The Changing Fortunes of Economic Liberalism

Yesterday, Today and Tomorrow
David Henderson
Occasional Paper 105 (new edition); ISBN 0 255 36520 9
£12.50

The Global Education Industry

Lessons from Private Education in Developing Countries
James Tooley
Hobart Paper 141 (new edition); ISBN 0 255 36503 9
£12.50

Saving Our Streams

*The Role of the Anglers' Conservation Association in
Protecting English and Welsh Rivers*
Roger Bate
Research Monograph 53; ISBN 0 255 36494 6
£10.00

Better Off Out?

The Benefits or Costs of EU Membership
Brian Hindley & Martin Howe
Occasional Paper 99 (new edition); ISBN 0 255 36502 0
£10.00

Buckingham at 25

Freeing the Universities from State Control
Edited by James Tooley
Readings 55; ISBN 0 255 36512 8
£15.00

Bastiat's *The Law*
Introduction by Norman Barry
Occasional Paper 123; ISBN 0 255 36509 8
£7.50

A Globalist Manifesto for Public Policy
Charles Calomiris
Occasional Paper 124; ISBN 0 255 36525 X
£7.50

Euthanasia for Death Duties
Putting Inheritance Tax Out of Its Misery
Barry Bracewell-Milnes
Research Monograph 54; ISBN 0 255 36513 6
£10.00

Liberating the Land
The Case for Private Land-use Planning
Mark Pennington
Hobart Paper 143; ISBN 0 255 36508 X
£10.00

IEA Yearbook of Government Performance 2002/2003
Edited by Peter Warburton
Yearbook 1; ISBN 0 255 36532 2
£15.00

Britain's Relative Economic Performance, 1870–1999
Nicholas Crafts
Research Monograph 55; ISBN 0 255 36524 1
£10.00

Should We Have Faith in Central Banks?
Otmar Issing
Occasional Paper 125; ISBN 0 255 36528 4
£7.50

The Dilemma of Democracy
Arthur Seldon
Hobart Paper 136 (reissue); ISBN 0 255 36536 5
£10.00

Capital Controls: a 'Cure' Worse Than the Problem?
Forrest Capie
Research Monograph 56; ISBN 0 255 36506 3
£10.00

The Poverty of 'Development Economics'

Deepak Lal

Hobart Paper 144 (reissue); ISBN 0 255 36519 5

£15.00

Should Britain Join the Euro?

The Chancellor's Five Tests Examined

Patrick Minford

Occasional Paper 126; ISBN 0 255 36527 6

£7.50

Post-Communist Transition: Some Lessons

Leszek Balcerowicz

Occasional Paper 127; ISBN 0 255 36533 0

£7.50

A Tribute to Peter Bauer

John Blundell et al.

Occasional Paper 128; ISBN 0 255 36531 4

£10.00

Employment Tribunals

Their Growth and the Case for Radical Reform

J. R. Shackleton

Hobart Paper 145; ISBN 0 255 36515 2

£10.00

Climate Alarmism Reconsidered
Robert L. Bradley Jr
Hobart Paper 146; ISBN 0 255 36541 1
£12.50

Government Failure: E. G. West on Education
Edited by James Tooley & James Stanfield
Occasional Paper 130; ISBN 0 255 36552 7
£12.50

Waging the War of Ideas
John Blundell
Second edition
Occasional Paper 131; ISBN 0 255 36547 0
£12.50

Corporate Governance: Accountability in the Marketplace
Elaine Sternberg
Second edition
Hobart Paper 147; ISBN 0 255 36542 X
£12.50

The Land Use Planning System
Evaluating Options for Reform
John Corkindale
Hobart Paper 148; ISBN 0 255 36550 0
£10.00

Economy and Virtue
Essays on the Theme of Markets and Morality
Edited by Dennis O'Keeffe
Readings 59; ISBN 0 255 36504 7
£12.50

Free Markets Under Siege
Cartels, Politics and Social Welfare
Richard A. Epstein
Occasional Paper 132; ISBN 0 255 36553 5
£10.00

Unshackling Accountants
D. R. Myddelton
Hobart Paper 149; ISBN 0 255 36559 4
£12.50

The Euro as Politics
Pedro Schwartz
Research Monograph 58; ISBN 0 255 36535 7
£12.50

Pricing Our Roads

Vision and Reality
Stephen Glaister & Daniel J. Graham
Research Monograph 59; ISBN 0 255 36562 4
£10.00

The Role of Business in the Modern World

Progress, Pressures, and Prospects for the Market Economy
David Henderson
Hobart Paper 150; ISBN 0 255 36548 9
£12.50

Public Service Broadcasting Without the BBC?

Alan Peacock
Occasional Paper 133; ISBN 0 255 36565 9
£10.00

The ECB and the Euro: the First Five Years

Otmar Issing
Occasional Paper 134; ISBN 0 255 36555 1
£10.00

Towards a Liberal Utopia?

Edited by Philip Booth
Hobart Paperback 32; ISBN 0 255 36563 2
£15.00

The Way Out of the Pensions Quagmire

Philip Booth & Deborah Cooper

Research Monograph 60; ISBN 0 255 36517 9
£12.50

To order copies of currently available IEA papers, or to enquire about availability, please contact:

Lavis Marketing
IEA orders
FREEPOST LON21280
Oxford OX3 7BR

Tel: 01865 767575
Fax: 01865 750079
Email: orders@lavismarketing.co.uk

The IEA also offers a subscription service to its publications. For a single annual payment, currently £40.00 in the UK, you will receive every title the IEA publishes during the course of a year, invitations to events, and discounts on our extensive back catalogue. For more information, please contact:

Adam Myers
Subscriptions
The Institute of Economic Affairs
2 Lord North Street
London SW1P 3LB

Tel: 020 7799 8920
Fax: 020 7799 2137
Website: www.iea.org.uk